NEW BIKE

Kate Petty

Photographs by Ed Barber

Start to Finish

Contents

A & C Black · London

A clever invention

The bicycle is a wonderfully simple and efficient machine. Five hundred years ago, the artist Leonardo da Vinci sketched a new idea for an invention with two wheels which someone could sit on and drive along. Nearly four hundred years later, the bicycle was invented.

One of the earliest cycles invented was the penny-farthing. It was made in 1871 and had a huge front wheel with pedals attached to it. The penny-farthing was faster than other bikes of the time, but it was a long way to fall off! Most bicycles that came afterwards had both wheels the same size. The back wheel was driven by the pedals and a chain, and the front wheel could be steered by turning the handlebars. From being a toy for rich people, the bicycle became the cheapest, quickest and most reliable way ordinary people could get around.

In 1888, the invention of the inflatable tyre made cycling more comfortable. So did the addition of gears, which made it easier to cycle uphill as well as enabling the cyclist to go faster on the flat.

The basic design of a bike has not changed from the last century although the handlebars might be a different shape or the wheels a different size. So how do bicycle manufacturers come up with new and exciting ways of selling bicycles? How can a buyer be persuaded to buy one bike rather than another?

This book looks at each stage of how a bike is made, from the first research to the finished bicycle ready for the shop.

Deciding on something different

How does a bike manufacturer predict what is going to be popular next?

The people in the marketing department talk to children and find out what they like and dislike. They look at fashions in sports and games. They find out which bikes are popular in America and Japan, and which are selling well in Britain and Europe. Sometimes they will just look at one feature of a best-selling bicycle, perhaps the handlebars or the saddle.

Penny works in the marketing department. She decides the sort of child the new bike will be aimed at. She needs to know how much money a parent is prepared to spend on a new bike.

Market research showed that mountain bikes and ATB's (All Terrain Bikes) were still very popular, but that most children rode on streets and pavements rather than cross-country. The children wanted their bikes to look good too.

Penny and the marketing department use this information to put together a description of what the new bike will be like. This list, called a brief, is used by the designers to make a new product. The company already make a bicycle called Extreme. The new bike will be called Even More Extreme!

PRODUCT MANAGEMENT/CONCEPT DESIGN

~~GRAPHIC~~ DESIGN BRIEF

Brand	RALEIGH
Model Name	EVEN MORE EXTREME
Colour Finish	NEON GREEN VAPOUR
Sample Availability	READY
TIMING	
Job 1 – Estimated	WEEK 23 (JUNE)
MODEL PURPOSE	TO PROVIDE A VISUALLY STUNNING ACTION BIKE. DEVELOP EXTREME AS A GENERIC BRAND IN THE MARKET – TO BECOME A CULT PRODUCT.
RANGE LOGIC	AN ALTERNATIVE TO BMX AND RALEIGH JUNIOR A.T.B. MODELS.
TARGET MARKET/ CONSUMER PROFILE	7 TO 10 YEAR OLD BOYS WHO ARE FASHION AWARE, WANT A BIKE THAT IS EYE-CATCHING AND DIFFERENT. SEEKING STREET CRED.
IMAGE POINTERS	TRENDSETTING, ASSERTIVE, WILDLY EXTREME, OUT-OF-THIS-WORLD
SPECIFICATION ASPECTS/ COMPONENT OPTIONS	* INDEX GEARS * BLACK WHEEL DISCS * SEMI-SLICK TYRES * AERO BLACK CHAINDISC
FRAME SIZES	13" FRAME WITH 20" WHEELS
KEY COMPETITORS	NONE AT £150.00 RETAIL PRICE NEAREST COMPETITORS ARE FORMULA 1 TYPE MODELS AT OVER £200.00

Originator A. Maxwell

Engineering design

John is an engineering designer. He makes a drawing of how the working parts of the bicycle will look.

The engineering designers are given the brief by the marketing department. They have to make sure the new bike will work well.

The frames for the bike will be made in the factory, but other parts, such as the saddles, wheels, and gears, may be bought from specialist manufacturers. The engineering designers look at catalogues to decide which ones will be the best for the new bicycle. Sometimes parts are made specially.

John's drawings are very accurate. He must be sure that the parts of the bike will fit together perfectly.

Computers are used to design the newest bikes. It is easier and quicker to change a design on a screen than on a detailed drawing. With a touch of his light pen John can change the length of the frame or take a close-up look at the gears.

John prints out a large-size drawing from his computer to give to the mechanical engineer so that a model can be built and used for testing. Some problems can be solved on the computer before a model is made. The first version of this bike didn't have the right number of links in the chain, so John had to change his drawing.

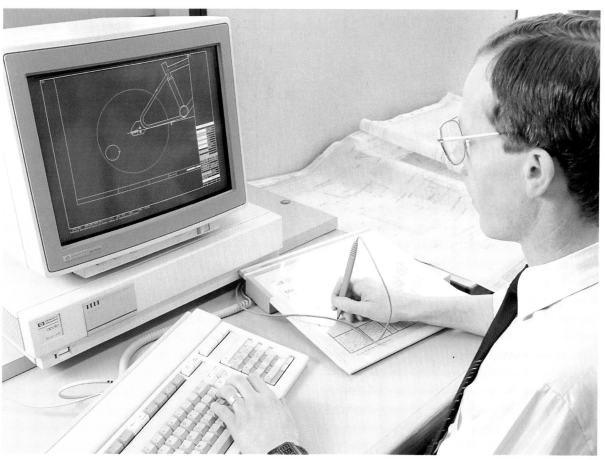

Graphic design

The graphic designers are in charge of the style and look of the bike. They need to make sure it will be fashionable. They keep up-to-date by visiting fashion shows and toy fairs. They find out which books children like to read and what television programmes are popular. They look in magazines and put together a scrapbook of the colours and ideas they think will be fashionable the following year.

Claire is a graphic designer. She tries out different lettering and colours to make the new bike look eye-catching.

The frame of the Even More Extreme is not very different from previous bikes. But the wheels are to have discs covering the spokes. This gives the designer a new area to cover with colour and words and patterns. She decides to decorate the discs with the name of the bike and some bright splashes of colour.

The designer tries out different colour schemes for the bike by spraying metal tubes with different paints. She can't always find the colour she wants: there isn't an unleaded paint which is really bright yellow. But bright green is no problem.

The designer types the name of the bike on to a computer which presses the letters out of sticky-backed plastic in a variety of different sizes. Claire sticks them on to a sample tube to see what they will look like.

Building a prototype

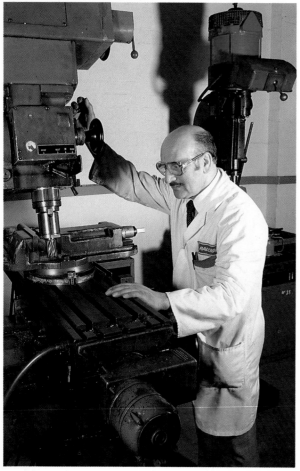

The bike can now be turned from a drawing into a real bicycle. The first models are called prototypes.

Ted makes the prototypes by hand, following the drawing given to him by the engineering designer. In his workshop, he cuts and shapes the metal parts he needs. He sees how they fit together before joining them permanently with a welding torch.

Ted's job is highly skilled. The work he does by hand on the prototype will be done in the factory when the bicycles are mass-produced.

The angles of the bicycle frame all have to be correct. Sometimes the tubes can bend whilst they are being welded because of the extreme heat, so Ted straightens them in a 'setting frame'.

When the frame has been put together, it is sent to be painted in the colours the designer has chosen. Then the parts which have come from other factories, such as the wheels and the saddle, are added.

The finished prototype looks exactly like the final bicycle. But it isn't too late to make changes. Ted can tell the designers if there are any changes which need to be made. Ted and his two colleagues can make a complete new bicycle in under four days.

Testing

The bicycle must be strong and safe to ride. All the parts of the new bike are individually tested. If they don't work or they aren't safe, they are not fitted on to the bike.

Paul works in the product test area. He tests the bike with machines that bend and twist it to simulate a person riding it. Some bikes are tested until they break to find out how many years they may last on the road.

In this 'saddle fatigue test', a pan shaped like a bottom rocks backwards and forwards to make sure that the saddle will not break or wear out.

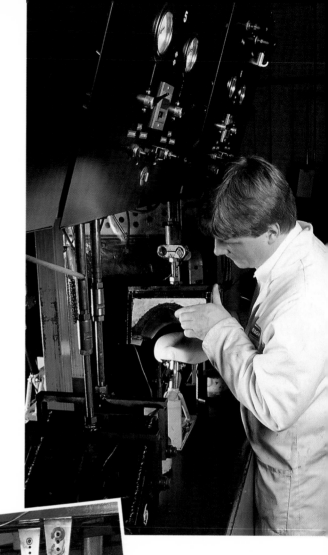

Then the bike is run for 250 hours at 40 kilometres per hour on rollers made like bumpy cobblestones.

All British bicycles have safety standards set by law. This is a British Safety Standards test which checks the strength of the handlebars. The results are shown on the dials attached to the testing machine and on a computer print-out.

Paul has to ride the bike for the 'braking distance test'. This test checks how quickly the bike stops when the brakes are used.

If the tests find any weaknesses in the prototype, they can be put right before the bike is manufactured in its thousands.

Getting the go-ahead

The prototype is finished and tested and ready for everyone to look at. The marketing people want to see if it matches their description. The graphic designers want to see how it looks. The engineering designers want to know if it works. Even local school children are invited in to give their views. Will it sell?

Everyone is very pleased with the new bike, especially the eye-catching wheel discs. But there is still a problem with the saddle. The cheaper one is less hard-wearing but the suppliers are local and can deliver quickly. The more expensive one is better quality but the order might arrive too late. Which one should they choose?

As soon as this problem has been solved, the factory gets ready for production. The gears in these boxes have been shipped all the way from Japan.

Space is cleared for large components such as wheel rims.

The factory staff use the production of the first fifty bikes as a trial run. The plastic wheel discs were a new feature and presented some difficulties. How can they be stored and handled? How easy is it to stick on the decorated transfers? Can the finished bike be packaged in the same way as other bikes?

Making the frame

The bicycle frame is made from hollow tubes of light steel. When the tubes arrive, they are as long as the lorries that carry them. At the 'tube shop' in the factory, a huge moving gantry lowers them in labelled bundles on to the correct racks.

The tubes are cut to the right length by a mechanical saw, then taken to the main factory to be joined together.

There are several different ways of joining the tubes. The frames of the Even More Extreme are welded together by a robot. The robot is programmed to put the welding torch in the right places. The parts of the frame are fitted to a rectangular 'jig' which flips over when one side has been completed so that the robot can weld the other side.

The finished frames have had holes drilled for attachments such as a water-bottle holder. The forks for the front wheel are welded separately and will not be attached to the bikes until they have been painted. The frames and forks are stacked ready to go to the 'paint shop'.

At the paint shop

The frames and forks are attached to conveyor lines. The lines carry them through all the painting processes.

First they are given an 'electrophoretic' coating, inside and out, which protects the metal from rust. Then they are dipped in an undercoat of grey paint.

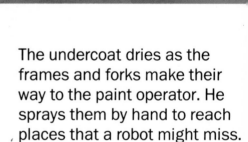

The undercoat dries as the frames and forks make their way to the paint operator. He sprays them by hand to reach places that a robot might miss.

The frames and forks continue their journey into the spray booth where a robot sprayer whirls paint at them.

Some types of bike have a special finish in a different colour which looks mottled. This is done by 'vaporizing'; the paint is sprayed on by hand as a powder.

All the frames and forks are baked dry in ovens like huge covered corridors. Each vaporized frame emerges bright and shiny and slightly different from the one next to it. The long lines hung with colourfully painted frames stretch like rainbows from one side of the factory to the other. When the frames and forks are dry, they are taken off the lines and stacked on trolleys.

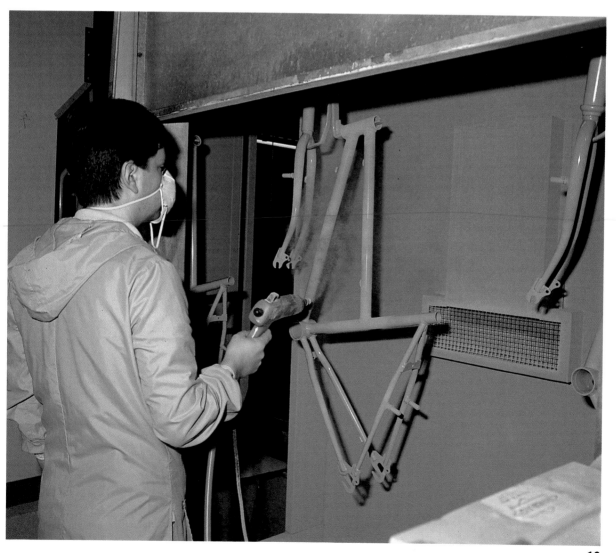

The wheels on the bike

Jean's job is to lace the spokes through the hub of each wheel. She can do this very quickly.

In the assembly part of the factory, the wheels are put together. When the spokes have been laced, they are put on a machine to fix them to the wheel rim. Spokes strengthen the wheel without making it heavy.

Next the tyre is fitted round the rim. An inner tube is pumped up a little and slipped in underneath. Then a machine blows compressed air into the tyre until it reaches the correct pressure.

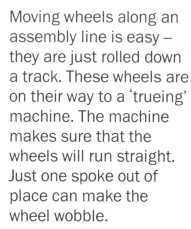

Moving wheels along an assembly line is easy – they are just rolled down a track. These wheels are on their way to a 'trueing' machine. The machine makes sure that the wheels will run straight. Just one spoke out of place can make the wheel wobble.

The assembly line

Every colourful transfer, with the Even More Extreme name on, must be stuck on by hand to the special black wheel discs.

Margaret fits the disc over the spokes and screws it into place.

Margaret carefully positions the transfer in the right place before sticking it down.

Now the wheels are ready for the assembly line.

The frame passes down a line of fourteen people. Each one adds a new part to the bike until it is complete.

First the front fork is screwed on to the frame, followed by the handlebars, complete with grips, brakes and a gear lever. Then the brake cables are attached.

The back wheel is fixed on before the front one, and the chain is fitted.

The saddle is one of the last parts to be added. The pedals are left for the new owners to fix for themselves. The bikes are made in batches of 500, and the factory usually produces about 20 000 bicycles a week.

Checking the quality

A badly-made bike could cause a serious accident. To prevent this, checks are made at every stage of a bike's production. When the bikes are finished, a number are picked from every batch and tested against a checklist. If there is a fault, the whole production line can be stopped. Fortunately, this rarely has to happen.

Clive works in quality control. He is often the first person to ride the finished bike. It's a good way of testing it. He has to put the pedals on before riding it round the factory.

The bikes are carefully packed in cardboard and polythene to stop them getting bumped or scratched before they are sold. The Even More Extremes need a special sort of packaging to prevent the wheel discs from being damaged. The bikes in the big picture are boxed in cardboard cartons. Every bike is labelled and hooked onto an overhead conveyor which carries them above the heads of the factory workers and onto the loading bay.

The delivery lorries reverse in a line right up to the loading bay so that the bikes don't have to go outside. Each bike has a label telling the packer which warehouse it will go to. From the warehouse, the bikes will be taken to shops all over the country.

Telling people about it

The advertising department have to think of the best way to tell children about the new product. For the Even More Extreme, they call in an advertising agency to help them. Together, they agree that lots of children choose a particular bike because a friend has one. The advertising department wants to persuade people that the Even More Extreme is the 'right bike' to be seen on.

They decide that the best way to persuade 7–10 year old boys is with a poster campaign. The advertising agency show several poster ideas to children. Nearly all of them like a cartoony poster best. The finished poster is put up in sports centres and shops at the beginning of the summer holidays. Extra posters are given away free inside comics such as *Beano* and *Dandy*.

Janet's job is to tell people about the new bikes in all sorts of ways. She persuades journalists to write about them in newspapers and magazines. She also helps to produce a catalogue which lists all the company's bicycles.

The advertising department also want a new idea to put in magazines which are read by the owners of bicycle shops. It needs to be something people will remember. The agency use the company logo of a heron, and add punky pink hair and dark glasses.

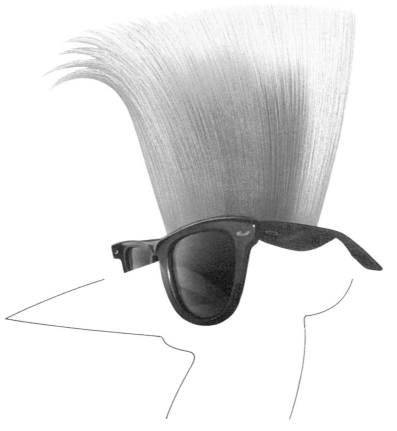

On sale

In February, a year after the bike was first thought of, the marketing department have a promotion to tell dealers about the Even More Extreme. The bikes appear in the shops from March. At first the Even More Extreme sells slowly, but as soon as the summer holiday poster campaign is under way, it becomes an enormous success.

Each new bike is sold with a handbook and a questionnaire. The results of the questionnaire help the marketing department to plan future new bikes. Some of the first bikes in the Extreme range were powdery blue but a lot of boys didn't like this colour, so purple bikes were made instead.

As the Even More Extreme has remained popular, new models have been added to the range, such as the Pretty Extreme and the Totally Extreme. What name would you give to a bike in the same range?

When the range is fully established, the company might produce accessories to go with it, such as caps, gloves, water-bottles and backpacks.

What next? Even when the bike is at the height of its popularity, the marketing department and designers are hard at work dreaming up the bike that will eventually replace it.

A quick look at how a bike is made

Marketing Department

Do market research to find out what children want. Produce brief. Check each stage.

Graphic Design

Decide on colour and style of new bike.

Engineering Design

Produce computer design of how bike will look.

Prototypes

Produce full size working model of bike.

Testing

Check to make sure new bike is safe and has no design faults.

Shop

Advertising Department

Advertise bike in magazines and comics and produce posters.

Warehouse

Orders come in. Bikes delivered by lorry.

Production

Frames welded.
Frames painted.
↓
Bike assembled.

Preparing for Production

Parts ordered. Wheels assembled. Discs fitted.

Quality Control

Test and check all stages of production.

Index

Published by A & C Black (Publishers) Limited
35 Bedford Row, London, WC1R 4JH

Text © 1991 Kate Petty
Photographs © 1991 Ed Barber

Acknowledgements

The author and publisher would like to thank everyone at Raleigh Industries Limited, especially Janet Burnett, for their help in the preparation of this book. The pictures of a penny farthing and an early bicycle are reproduced by kind permission of the National Motor Museum, Beaulieu. Thanks also to Day's Cycles of Wood Green.

A CIP catalogue record for this book is available from the British Library.

ISBN 0–7136–3482–0

Filmset by August Filmsetting, Haydock, St Helens
Printed in Belgium by Proost International Book Production